The **FATHERLESS** Journey
for Girls

A 30 Day Devotional Guide

Sean P. Teis

with **April M. Yeager**

The **FATHERLESS** Journey
for Girls

A 30 Day Devotional Guide

Sean P. Teis

with April M. Yeager

Life Factors Ministries
spreading hope for life

The Fatherless Journey For Girls
A 30 Day Devotional Guide

ISBN: 978-0-9832039-6-4

Life Factors Ministries
P.O. Box 213, Duncansville, PA 16635

info@lifefactors.org
www.lifefactors.org

Scripture quotations are taken from: The King James Version

Printed in the United States of America

Faithful Life Publishers and Printers
North Fort Myers, FL 33903

www.FaithfulLifePublishers.com
info@FLPublishers.com

18 17 16 15 14 13 12 11   1 2 3 4 5

THE FATHERLESS JOURNEY

TO

_____

FROM

_____

DATE

_____

The Fatherless Journey

TRIP SCHEDULE

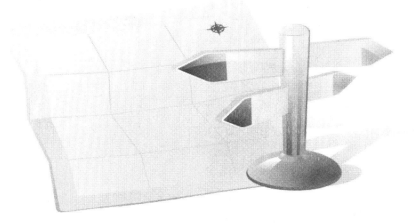

Preparation

Day 1 – Your Heavenly Father
Day 2 – So, You Are Fatherless
Day 3 – Facing the Facts
Day 4 – Talking to God
Day 5 – You Are Not Alone
Day 6 – You Are Loved
Day 7 – Consequences for Not Going
Day 8 – Overcoming Fear
Day 9 – Dealing with Discouragement

The Trip – Week 1 – The Beginning (Internal Change)

Day 10 – Forgiveness
Day 11 – Inferiority
Day 12 – Trusting God
Day 13 – Giving It All to God
Day 14 – Outer Beauty
Day 15 – Inner Beauty
Day 16 – Purity of Mind and Heart

The Trip – Week 2 – The Middle (External Change)
Day 17 – Purity of Body
Day 18 – Finding Godly Friendships
Day 19 – Submission to Authority
Day 20 – Finding Security
Day 21 – Father's Day
Day 22 – Breaking the Cycle
Day 23 – Being an Example

The Trip – Week 3 – The End (Your Future)
Day 24 – Be Confident
Day 25 – Mentors
Day 26 – A Biblical Marriage
Day 27 – Finding Wisdom
Day 28 – Woman of God
Day 29 – Setting Goals
Day 30 – Success

WELCOME

Hello!

Welcome to the Fatherless Journey! Most likely you did not decide to go on this journey, but for some reason out of your control, some circumstance brought you to this position in your life. When you became fatherless, regardless of how young it was, the feelings were probably as if someone gave you a suitcase that weighed a thousand pounds and told you to start walking. Included in this journey there were no instructions, no estimation of how long it would take, and really not much help at all. So, now you are here, you may feel all alone, looking at this journey and thinking to yourself, how will I complete this thing?

Wel,l there is good news; this devotional is designed to help you along your individual journey. There are certain issues you are facing or will come to face within being fatherless and they need to be addressed. You need preparation, because the trip isn't going to be easy, and it isn't always fun, but with a little help and guidance you can make it through it. I did it, and I have several friends that have as well. I have taken the knowledge of my personal experience and have polled others, and the next 30 days we will focus on the key elements that will most likely bog you down on your journey.

CHOICES – CHOICES – CHOICES

So now you have the following two choices:

1. You can lie down and be defeated and never conquer this journey, dealing with the consequences for the rest of your life.

-OR-

2. You can get started, conquer this life circumstance, and put this journey behind you as much as possible.

That is right, it is your decision. You as an individual decide what path you will take for the rest of your life, and you must get through this journey in order to move on. You can't ignore it, because it is staring you right in the face. To live a successful life you must confront this situation, and begin dealing with it, and I hope that you will. I am positive you will make the right decision, and I cannot wait until I see you on the other side of this mountain. Have a great trip!

Oh, I almost forgot to mention, you will not be going on this trip alone. Marie will be your guide. She has experience with this journey and even personally had to travel on it at the same age that you are right now. Each day Marie will share some insight on that day's specific topic. She will show you that since she got through it, you can too. She is ready, excited, and waiting to go on this trip with you!

You know you too have the ability to conquer this journey and continue on successfully with the rest of your life. What are you waiting for? Go ahead and begin with day 1. I will be praying for you!

Your Friend,

Sean Teis
President
Life Factors Ministries

P.S. If you have any questions or need help along your journey please contact me through email at seanteis@lifefactors.org or on Facebook at http://www.facebook.com/SeanTeis, and I will try my best to help.

The Fatherless Journey

MYFATHERLESSJOURNEY.ORG

Life Factors Ministries created myfatherlessjourney.org as a website specifically designed to meet the needs of all fatherless girls/guys, single moms/guardians, and mentors. We are here for you and want to help you along your fatherless journey! Check out the site today!

PREPARATION

Days 1-9

The Fatherless Journey

Day 1

<u>Your Heavenly Father</u>

"For God so loved the world, that He gave His only begotten Son, that whosoever believeth in Him should not perish, but have everlasting life." John 3:16

I am so excited to finally meet you. This trip will be exciting, but it will not be easy. I am confident that you will be able to conquer the certain areas in your life that will need improvement, and I want you to know that I will be with you the entire time. I will share with you some insight into my personal fatherless journey with hope that it will help and encourage you. The most amazing information that anyone has ever shared with me was the fact that God sent His only Son to this world to save me from my sins. The most important decision that I ever made was by asking Jesus Christ into my heart as my personal Savior. How wonderful it is to know for sure that I will go to Heaven when I die. You too have the ability to decide where you will go when you die. If you have never accepted Christ as your personal Savior, follow the steps on the next page in the challenge section. Your decision of where you will spend eternity is the most important decision that you will ever make.

-Marie

CHALLENGE - Day 1

Where you will go when you die is the most important decision you will ever make. That is right; it is your decision. You also get to decide whether or not you want a relationship with your Heavenly Father. You most likely did not decide to be fatherless, but now you have a chance to reconcile that event by seeking your Heavenly Father. The first step on the Fatherless Journey is confirming that you have a relationship with the Lord Jesus Christ. God wants you to rest in Him as your Heavenly Father. He will never leave, and He will never forsake you (Hebrews 13:5). All you must do is accept His Son, the Lord Jesus Christ as your personal Savior. John 3:16 above shows that God loved us so much that He made a way for us to go to Heaven by sending His only begotten Son. The following verses will show you how to accept this free gift that He is offering to you:

> **1. Romans 3:23** – You must realize that you are a sinner. Have you ever lied, cheated, used a curse word, or disrespected your elder? If so, then you have sinned before, and admitting you are a sinner is the first step. Every person has sinned.
> **2. Romans 6:23a** – The punishment for your sin is eternal death in Hell.
> **3. Romans 5:8** – Out of God's love for us, He sent His Son to die for our sins. This is our hope, through Christ we can be saved from an eternal death.
> **4. Romans 6:23b** – God's gift is eternal life in Heaven through Jesus Christ.
> **5. Romans 10:13** – You must accept the gift by faith believing in Jesus and asking Him to come into your heart. If you understand this information and would like to ask Jesus into your heart, please pray the suggested prayer below.

 ACTION - In My Prayer Journal

In your first prayer journal entry, write out a thank you letter to God for sending His Son to die for your sins.

Suggested Prayer: Dear Lord Jesus, I know that I am a sinner. I know that You are God, and I know that You died in my place to pay for my sin. I believe that You rose from the dead, proving that You are God. Right now, in the best way that I know how, I call upon You and ask You to be my Lord and my Savior and my God. Thank You Jesus for dying for me. Help me now to live for You. Amen.

The Fatherless Journey

The Fatherless Journey

Day 2
<u>So, You Are Fatherless</u>

"Not that I speak in respect of want: for I have learned, in whatsoever state I am, therewith to be content." Philippians 4:11

When I think of the title, *So You Are Fatherless*, I think about different types of situations. Some may have lost their father due to death, others may have a father that is physically present but not actually there, or if you are like me, you are fatherless because your father has decided to be absent from your life. Regardless of how you became fatherless, you are fatherless. When I was a teenager, I remember ignoring the fact that I was actually fatherless until one day when I heard Psalm 27:10 "When my father and my mother forsake me, then the LORD will take me up. " After hearing this verse, I realized that I did not have to be alone. God was there and ready to take me into his arms and love me as a father should. Upon this realization the void felt filled; even though I did not have a physical presence of a father, I knew my Father was there. Even the best earthly father is still just a man, and they have the potential of letting their daughters down, but I can always rely on my God the Father. The same God that became my Father is waiting with open arms to be your father too.

-Marie

CHALLENGE - Day 2

Let's face it, just being fatherless is sometimes quite depressing, compiled with the many life-altering results of fatherlessness it may at times make you feel hopeless. You may be asking yourself several questions such as: Who will protect my family? Who will help me make something of myself? Who will teach me about men? The reality is that you may not have someone to consistently teach you, but you have been given a far different unique life path. You have been given the opportunity to learn from several men and women a variety of life lessons. You have been given independence and trust in many areas of your life and in the many decisions that you will face. Being fatherless is not a fun situation, and it definitely is hard to face, but you can get through it. As you prepare for this journey, start thinking about contentment. What are the things in your life that you could be thankful for? What are things in your life that could be worse? You must accept the situation that you have been given and learn to be content. Follow today's theme verse and begin to practice contentment in whatever life may bring: Philippians 4:11 "Not that I speak in respect of want: for I have learned, in whatsoever state I am, therewith to be content."

 ## ACTION - In My Prayer Journal

Write out the things that you have to be thankful for and content about in your life. Remember that your life can always be in a worse position than it currently is.

Suggested Prayer: Dear God, help me to be content in this fatherless situation of my life. Help me to be thankful for the things that You have given to me and not to worry about the things I am missing. I thank You today for the blessings that You have given me, and I pray that You would give me strength for the shortcomings. Amen.

The Fatherless Journey

The Fatherless Journey

Day 3

<u>Facing the Facts</u>

"For I know the thoughts that I think toward you, saith the LORD, thoughts of peace, and not of evil, to give you an expected end." Jeremiah 29:11

The facts of fatherlessness are scary stuff! Check out some of the statistics that are being said about you and me:

> "90% of homeless and runaway children are from fatherless homes."[1]

> "Children who lived with only one parent had lower grade point averages, lower college aspirations, poor attendance records, and higher dropout rates than students who lived with both parents."[2]

> "Fatherless Children are at a dramatically greater risk of drug and alcohol abuse, mental illness, suicide, poor educational performance, teen pregnancy, and criminality."[3]

After reading these statistics I am very thankful that I did not become one of them. In high school I read the book called *This Present Darkness* by Frank Perretti. Through this book my eyes were opened at the joy that Satan receives through his victories over individuals. As I ponder on these statistics, I realize that he takes pleasure in them. He is the master of deceit, and he deceives us in many ways. The following are just a few of the ways he deceives fatherless young ladies:

1. He makes us think that it is our fault that we are fatherless.
2. He makes us think that we will find security in other men.
3. He makes us think that we should blame God.

You need to realize that if you choose to follow God and His truth and reject Satan and his lies, you will have the ability to rise above the statistics and God can fulfill His plan in your life.

-Marie

CHALLENGE - Day 3

These facts are very shocking and could be influential in your life. The true fact is that you have the opportunity to not be one of the statistics. The act of a father leaving is detrimental to anyone. It has most likely affected your actions, attitude, thought process, and many other attributes of your life. After becoming fatherless the most important necessity is to rely on God to get you through it. The wonderful thing about being a Christian is that you do not have to become a statistic. Romans 8:17 shows us that though we may suffer certain obstacles in this world, we have the hope of someday being "glorified together" in Heaven. Following this in verse 28 we are shown that "All things work together for good to them that love God." The Special Olympics are people of all ages who had the facts stacked against them. Many are labeled as disabled or handicapped, but this label does not stop them from pursuing their dreams of being an athlete. Some have an intellectual disability, others have a physical deformity and the Special Olympics is a way for them to display their willingness to persevere despite their disabilities. You have not chosen to be a fatherless statistic, but you have the ability to be who God wants you to be on this earth, regardless of the statistics that you may face. You may suffer in this world, being fatherless, but if you live for the Lord despite your circumstances glory will eventually come and all things will work together. Through your relationship with Jesus Christ you are able to conquer the biggest obstacles in this world.

 # ACTION - In My Prayer Journal

Write out a challenge for yourself of how you will not become one of the statistics. Challenge yourself with goals that can be easily accomplished. Continuously look back at your goals and confirm that you are still accomplishing them.

Suggested Prayer: Dear Lord, thank You for giving me hope in You, that despite the circumstance I may face on this earth. I will be glorified together with You someday. I thank You for giving me the understanding that all things will work together through You. Please give me strength to face the facts of this trial in my life. Amen.

The Fatherless Journey

The Fatherless Journey

Day 4

Talking to God

"The effectual fervent prayer of a righteous man availeth much." James 5:16b

There were two minutes left on the clock, the score was 3-2. Our girls' soccer team was about to beat a team that had never been beaten by our school before. I was the goalie, and the opponent was fiercely trying to score a goal on me, but we persevered and won the game. We had just beaten a team that had never been beaten in the history of our school! Years later, after having my own children, I still love to talk to former teammates about the great memories of this game and other games we had played. I remember loving the game and having great memories of victory and of defeat. Despite a win or a loss, my friends and I would reminisce about the events during the game whether it was sadness of goals given up or excitement over great plays that were made. This is the type of friendship that God wants to have with us. He wants to hear about our good times and bad times. Sometimes people do not show their emotion to God, because they think that God already knows about these things. I have found that many people only use prayer in desperate times, such as when a loved one is sick, when financial problems hit, or when their world seems upside down. The truth is that God wants to be our friend through every situation of life. I challenge you to have daily talks with God through the good and the bad. If you haven't tried out the journal in the back of this book, check it out today, and don't be afraid to share everything that is on your mind and heart.

-Marie

CHALLENGE - Day 4

Today there are multiple resources for communication. We can email, chat, text, talk on the phone, communicate on social sites such as Facebook, Twitter, and MySpace, and many other avenues. With all of these resources at our fingertips, there are times when we still may feel like we have no one to talk to. Do you ever just want someone to talk to? Why not talk to God? Talking to God is simple. You do not have to login, dial a number, or click send, but rather you just have to begin speaking to Him. He is always there, and He is always willing to listen to you. David is a great Biblical example of someone that continuously talked to God through the good and the bad times of life. The book of Psalms is filled with conversations that David had with God. These conversations reveal David's ups and downs in his life. Some Psalms are happy and some are sad. The Bible shows us in I Samuel 13:14 and Acts 13:22 that David was a man after God's own heart. David loved to talk to God. David was not perfect, but he laid his burdens down at God's feet. What about you? Who do you talk to in the good and bad times? Who will you talk to in the times to come? James 5:16b tells us that "The effectual fervent prayer of a righteous man availeth much." This means that talking to God will bring into your life great gain.

 # ACTION - In My Prayer Journal

Write a note to God thanking Him for the things He has done and is doing in your life. Talk to Him about your burdens and problems. Look back at this note often and see what God has done in your life.

Suggested Prayer: Dear Lord, I thank You for loving me and giving me the ability to call upon You whenever I want. I ask that You would guide me as I begin to talk to You more. Please give me strength to get through my fatherless struggles, realizing that You are always there to listen to me. Amen.

The Fatherless Journey

The Fatherless Journey

Day 5

<u>You Are Not Alone</u>

"Let your conversation be without covetousness; and be content with such things as ye have: for He hath said, I will never leave thee, nor forsake thee." Hebrews 13:5

When I was on my journey I did not have a guide to help me. That is why I have given my life to go on this journey with fellow fatherless friends. Have you thought about what will happen after you have finished this devotional book and I am not there to guide you anymore? One important item I want you to not forget is that you are not alone. Repeat after me, "I Am Not Alone." If you followed Day 1 or previously asked Jesus into your heart, you will never be alone. You and I have a friend in Jesus that is always there. No matter what time of the day we can talk to Him, ask Him for comfort, and seek advice from Him. Jesus loves you and wants you to succeed on this journey! When I was in high school attending youth group one night my youth pastor told us an interesting story. Here is a summary of that story:

His father was on a mission's trip in Haiti. They were driving through the jungle one night in a pickup truck. His father was in the back of the pickup truck. Suddenly several Haitian natives appeared from out of nowhere and began to surround their vehicle. These natives where chanting evil sayings. It was evident that these men were evil and were out to destroy these missionary workers. In fear and trembling the missionaries began singing "There Is Power In The Blood." These evil natives, now pressed up against the vehicle began to back away and in an instance they disappeared.

Though I heard this story such a long time ago it still amazes me, because it shows that God is always with us. It proves that no matter how alone you or I may feel we are actually not alone at all. As Christians, God is always near. We have the Power of the Blood of Jesus Christ to get us through anything. I challenge you today to rest in the Power of the Blood.

–Marie

CHALLENGE - Day 5

Do you ever feel like you are all alone on your own personal island, as if no one understands you and your situation, or as if you are the only person going through this fatherless experience on planet earth? When the word island is mentioned today many individuals think of the old famous television show, Gilligan's Island. If you have never heard of this show before, it was about a group of individuals that were stranded on a deserted island, displaying in a comical format how they survived and their attempts to get off of the island. The following is part of their theme song:

Just sit right back and you'll hear a tale, a tale of a fateful trip
That started from this tropic port, aboard this tiny Ship.
The mate was a mighty sailin' man, the Skipper brave and sure,
Five passengers set sail that day for a three hour tour.
A three hour tour.
The weather started getting rough, the tiny ship was tossed.
If not for the courage of the fearless crew, the Minnow would be lost.
The Minnow would be lost...[4]

Though you may feel like Gilligan, all alone on your individual island, you must realize you are never alone. Hebrews 13:5 assures us of this in saying, "for He hath said I will never leave thee nor forsake thee." When you feel most alone remember God is near to you!

 # ACTION - In My Prayer Journal

Make a list of the times you feel most alone. Begin to ask God to give you strength and comfort in those times.

Suggested Prayer: Dear Lord, please help me today to be aware of Your presence. Help me to remember that You are near when I may feel alone, because Your Scriptures say You will never leave me nor forsake me. Amen.

The Fatherless Journey

The Fatherless Journey

Day 6

You Are Loved

"I am crucified with Christ: nevertheless I live; yet not I, but Christ liveth in me: and the life which I now live in the flesh I live by the faith of the Son of God, who loved me, and gave Himself for me." Galatians 2:20

Do you ever feel unloved? It is common to feel this way when you are fatherless. When I was growing up, I used to be overcome with jealousy towards those who did have fathers. Some of my friends would talk about going on dates with their dads or doing some type of activity with them, and I would not have anything to say. Also, people used to ask me what it was like growing up fatherless, and before I could respond they would say, "Well I guess you do not know what you missed." This question was somewhat ridiculous. How would I not know what I missed? I knew that I did not have someone to call daddy, to protect me, to hug me, or to love me like a daddy loves his little girl. I knew this fact, and I did not know what to do about it, but one day it was revealed to me that God loved me. He loves me like a daddy loves his little girl. It is true God does love us. He loved us so much that He sent His own Son to die for us. You cannot change your father and his mistakes, but you can change how you look at your situation. Though our earthly father may not show love to us, our Heavenly Father loves us more than we need in Jeremiah 31:3 it says, "Yea, I have loved thee with an everlasting love." I challenge you today to not forget how much you are loved!

-Marie

CHALLENGE - Day 6

Think to yourself for a moment about what you believe love really is. Many people differ on their opinion of love. For all of us love is a needed act or gift toward us. When we know we are loved our day is better and the sun seems to shine a little brighter. What happens though when we do not feel loved? This is one of the most crucial parts of a fatherless individual's life. Many of the bad statistics resulting from fatherlessness have a direct connection from the lack of love in the child or teens life. No matter how unloved you may feel at times you should be comforted to know that Christ loves you. He loved you so much that He was crucified on a cross, stabbed in the side with a sword, spat upon, forced to wear a crown of thorns, mocked, and ultimately persecuted for most of his life. He loves us so much that He died for us. Galatians 2:20 tells us that as Christians we are crucified with Christ. Many times our lives will not be easy, but we can rest assured that no matter what problems we will face we have the ability to get through them simply by resting in the love of Christ.

 ACTION - In My Prayer Journal

Write a letter to Jesus thanking Him for His love and for what He has done in your life.

Suggested Prayer: Dear Lord, I thank You for dying for me and for giving me hope of eternity in Heaven with You! I love You and thank You for loving me! Amen.

The Fatherless Journey

The Fatherless Journey

Day 7

Consequences for Not Going

"Wherefore he saith, Awake thou that sleepest, and arise from the dead, and Christ shall give thee light. See then that ye walk circumspectly, not as fools, but as wise, Redeeming the time, because the days are evil. Wherefore be ye not unwise, but understanding what the will of the Lord is." Ephesians 5:14-17

There are only two more days of preparation until we begin our trip. I am excited as I am sure you are. As we have been preparing have you had any thoughts about not going? I am sure that you have. I know I did. Since the journey is so difficult and there are so many obstacles, at this point, many individuals either postpone the trip for an extended period of time or never make it at all. I traveled on this journey for a long time even throughout my high school years, but to my regret after high school I stopped. I stopped moving forward because of self-pity. I was in debt, I got into a wrong relationship, and I took my eyes off of God and tried to live through my own self-sufficiency. One bad decision led to another, and I just found myself continuing to wander further and further away from my relationship with God. I quit trying. This left me with feelings of regret, emptiness, and the feeling of knowing that I had let my Heavenly Father down. The statistics are not a joke and failing to conquer this journey in your life may lead you to becoming one of them. I want to challenge you as we continue preparing and then as we finally begin the trip, to not give up, because the consequences are too great to bear, and they will affect you for the rest of your life.

-Marie

CHALLENGE - Day 7

There is an old saying: "Hindsight sees 20/20," which basically means that if you would have known the consequences or rewards of something you did before you did it, you may have changed your actions. Jonah is a famous Bible character from the Old Testament that ultimately displays the meaning of this old saying. Jonah was told by God that he was to go to Nineveh, but due to his hatred towards the people of Nineveh, he ran from God and did go on the journey that was laid before him. The consequences for Jonah not going on this trip were tremendous; he was swallowed by a great fish. He should be in the <u>Guinness Book of World Records</u> for being the only man to ever be inside a great fish's belly and live to tell about it. If Jonah would have had hindsight he would have never tried to run from God. Being inside the great fish's belly and then being thrown up by the whale was most likely not a glamorous experience. Once Jonah saw that the only option was to serve the Lord he began to walk in God's steps. His life was quickly used by God to reach individuals. Ephesians 5:14-17 shows us that we must redeem the time that God has given to us. We must walk in the Lord's will and He will give us light. At this point in your life God's desire for you is to conquer this journey. Do not give up for the consequences are too great, and you might get eaten by a great fish!

 ACTION - In My Prayer Journal

Make a list of the top 5 things that you know God wants you to do with your life right now. Some examples would be: respecting your parents, conquering this journey, living a pure life, giving 100% in school, witnessing to a friend, quitting a bad habit, etc.

Suggested Prayer: Dear Lord, only through You and Your strength can I conquer this journey in my life. Please help me today to seek You and Your strength through any life circumstances that I may face. Amen.

The Fatherless Journey

The Fatherless Journey

Day 8

<u>Overcoming Fear</u>

"For God hath not given us the spirit of fear; but of power, and of love, and of a sound mind." II Timothy 1:7

When I was 10 years old I got really sick, enough to where my mom took me to the hospital. After a brief stay at the hospital, the doctors discharged me advising that it was only a minor infection that would heal itself in a few days. However, I went home and started to feel worse than I did at the hospital. My mother took me back to hospital due to the decline in my health. Once I went back in and after the doctors had re-examined me, they were nervous to report to my mom that they had misdiagnosed my sickness and that my appendix had ruptured. If I would have waited one more day to go back to the hospital, I could have died. As scary as this situation was, God was in control and I did not need to fear what would happen to me. After a few weeks in the hospital, I was feeling much better and able to go home. God helped me overcome this fearful circumstance and many other fearful situations that I have faced in my life. God will help you through your fearful circumstances as well. I challenge you today to not let any of your fears get in your way; seek God for help in conquering your fears. God is here for you.

-Marie

CHALLENGE - Day 8

September 11, 2001, is a historic day for the United States. Many individuals remember exactly what they were doing when they heard of the events that were taking place. It was a shock to the nation. Many heroes came about from this historic day, due to their efforts in acting in time of need. One such man was named Todd Beamer. Todd boarded Flight United 93 going from Newark, NJ to San Francisco, CA. His flight was on one of the planes that were hijacked that day by terrorists and instead of going to San Francisco as he had planned; his flight was being re-routed to Washington DC. Todd and a few other passengers on the plane knew that they had to do something. They could not just sit in their seats with fear and allow these terrorists to complete their mission. Todd's last audible words were, "Are you guys ready? Let's roll." The group conquered fear and took over the plane which soon came crashing down in a field in Somerset, Pennsylvania. Though none of the passengers on that flight survived that day, Todd became known as a national hero, because he gave his life to save others. They overcame their fear and conquered the obstacles that were set in front of them. [5] II Timothy 1:7 shows us that fear is not from God. Fear limits us from living to our fullest potential. What are you fearful of? II Timothy 1:7 also shows us that God hath given us power, love, and a sound mind. When you become fearful, remember that we have power through the Lord; trust Him today to help you overcome your fear.

 # ACTION - In My Prayer Journal

Write out a list of all of your fears. Begin meditating on II Timothy 1:7 daily thinking of your fears, and ask God to help you conquer them.

Suggested Prayer: Dear Lord, I realize only through You am I able to overcome my fears. I ask that from this day forward You will strengthen me to live with power, love, and a sound mind. Amen.

The Fatherless Journey

The Fatherless Journey

Day 9

Dealing with Discouragement

"Cast thy burden upon the LORD, and He shall sustain thee: He shall never suffer the righteous to be moved." Psalm 55:22

Well, we are finally here. Today is the last day of preparation and tomorrow begins week 1 of our trip. Have you felt any discouragement during preparation, or have you been discouraged about the trip in any way? If you have, it is completely normal. You are trying to conquer one of the hardest obstacles you will ever face in your life. When I was your age, I used to constantly deal with discouragement. Fatherlessness and discouragement go hand-in-hand. I used to be discouraged about my grades, sports, appearance, abilities, and much more. It was always hard to not worry about what people thought about me. People with good dads are usually very confident because their fathers instill confidence and encouragement into them. I remember being at an indoor soccer tournament and I was beginning to get discouraged during the game. After this discouragement came over me, a man from my church and a father of one of the girls on my team began saying some encouraging words to me, though he may not have realized it, this meant a lot. Another time I remember being at a camp as a CIT (Counselor In Training) and one of my pastors gave me words of encouragement, telling me he was proud of how I was working, again this meant a lot to me. These two men and a few others during my teen years helped me with my discouragement, but I was able to really begin conquering discouragement when I fully realized that through God I am sufficient. I challenge you today to cast your burdens on the Lord for only He will be able to help you deal with your discouragement!

-Marie

CHALLENGE - Day 9

The yells, sounds of marching, and sounds of chariots were drawing nigh. They were getting very nervous and fearful that they were going to be taken captive again and possibly even murdered. Suddenly, Moses lifted his rod toward the Heavens, trusting that God would save them, and the miracle of the Red Sea parting took place. The waters drew back from side to side providing a pathway to walk free and clear, and as soon as they were all across, the waters came tumbling down destroying the soldiers that sought destruction upon their lives. (Exodus 14). God had delivered them from their discouragement and at the end of this trial the Bible says, "And Israel saw that great work which the LORD did upon the Egyptians: and the people feared the LORD, and believed the LORD, and his servant Moses." Exodus 14:31. This is just one example of the many times Moses cast burdens upon the Lord for himself and the Israelites during their journey through the wilderness to the Promised Land, and He miraculously delivered them. No matter the circumstances they faced, God sustained them! Psalm 55:22 tells us to "Cast thy burden upon the LORD, and He shall sustain thee." Only God is able to help us in every moment of our life. By allowing God to deal with your discouragement, you too shall be able to look back and see what great things He has done for you. Deal with your discouragement by giving it to God today!

 ACTION - In My Prayer Journal

Make a list of the items you are currently discouraged about in your life. Pray over them and then begin praying for 30 days straight that God would deliver you from discouragement.

Suggested Prayer: Dear Lord, I give You my burdens. I ask that in this time of discouragement in my life that You would sustain me. I trust You and love You! Amen.

The Fatherless Journey

THE TRIP - WEEK 1

Days 10-16

The Fatherless Journey

Day 10

Forgiveness

"Let all bitterness, and wrath, and anger, and clamour, and evil speaking, be put away from you, with all malice: And be ye kind one to another, tenderhearted, forgiving one another, even as God for Christ's sake hath forgiven you."

Ephesians 4:31-32

When I was in college I wrote a letter to my birth father telling him that I was not bitter against him for abandoning my family and everything else that he had done. I did this because I came to the realization that the Bible says if I do not forgive others then God would not forgive me. This was revealed to me through Matthew 6:15 "But if ye forgive not men their trespasses, neither will your Father forgive your trespasses."

Despite the fact that he had not supported me emotionally, financially, or mentally and completely abandoned me, I decided to still forgive him. He never offered any repentance toward me, but I still knew that I had to forgive him. Through my action of forgiveness God allowed some great things to happen:

> 1. I had incredible peace from God.
> 2. My birth father realized that I did not have any resentment towards him and in return began trying to have a relationship with me.

Although he did put a little effort in establishing a relationship with me, it did not last, because he has trapped himself in a life path that keeps him from happiness. However, I am encouraged to know that he now knows that I am not bitter at him. I challenge you to forgive your father or anyone else that you may have bitterness towards in your life.

-Marie

CHALLENGE - Day 10

You cannot escape the reality that in life there are times when you must forgive people. Since no man is perfect, they are prone to, at times, bring hurt and disappointment. Forgiveness is a major step towards success in every fatherless child's life. You must forgive in order to continue on a successful journey. This is the first day of your trip and today you must make a very crucial decision. You may be thinking to yourself that you have already forgiven your father, and that the step of forgiveness has already been taken in your life. Aside from forgiveness of your father, you may need to forgive others as well. A lot of times there is bitterness and anger stored up that needs released. This bitterness and anger can be directed toward your father, but also toward your mother, siblings, step mother, step dad, someone that has neglected you, someone that you may think caused your father to leave, even anger towards God, or towards someone that has not been mentioned. When forgiveness is ignored there are always consequences to pay. This consequence could be a broken relationship or a demolished future due to bitterness and anger, a lack of trust in other relationships, and many other things. When bitterness is planted in your life, it brings about growth that is against God. Many times, bitterness causes people to fight, bicker, hate, and even murder. Making this first step on your journey may be the hardest you will take. For some it may involve several steps; meaning that you have more than one person to forgive, but you need to start somewhere.

THE BASIS FOR FORGIVENESS: When Jesus died on the cross for you, He performed the ultimate act of forgiveness. He forgave you for every sin that you have committed and every sin that you will commit in the future. When Christ shed His blood on the cross it was for you to be forgiven of your sins. Just as Christ forgave you, you are responsible to forgive others. You are also responsible to ask forgiveness of any wrong doings that you do to others. There are four steps to this part of the journey.

1. Forgive Your Dad
2. Forgive Yourself
3. Forgive Others, and Ultimately
4. Ask God for Forgiveness

You must work through these 4 levels of forgiveness as you travel on the fatherless journey, or you will not be able to successfully conquer this struggle in your life.

ACTION - In My Prayer Journal

Make a list of the individuals in your life that you need to forgive. Begin to pray for them and ask God to forgive you for any bitterness, hatred, or anger that you may feel. Then daily seek His strength and guidance to love those that have hurt you.

Suggested Prayer: Dear Lord, please forgive me for not being forgiving to those who have hurt me or who have caused me pain. Please forgive me for my bitterness or anger, and please help me to forgive and love my father, myself, and others and to put You first in my life. Amen.

The Fatherless Journey

The Fatherless Journey
Day 11

Inferiority

"Not that we are sufficient of ourselves to think anything as of ourselves; but our sufficiency is of God." II Corinthians 3:5

As a teenager you become overwhelmed with inferiority. How do I look? What are people saying about me? What do guys think of me? How can I be cool? I remember having all these thoughts as well when I was a teenager. Many of which streamed from fatherlessness. I always thought to myself how wonderful it would have been to have a father to guide me. I went to a private Christian school and I was among the small percentage that had divorced parents. I would watch my friends with wondrous thoughts about the fact that they had a dad and I did not. They had the opportunity to learn the key essentials about life from a father, and I did not. They had a man to protect them to show them how a man should treat them and love them, and I did not. The good news is that it does not last forever. I remember recently talking to one of my best friends from high school and laughing about how we were always worried about so many things in school, and now, none of those matters. Although it may not seem like it now, these years will go by quickly, and you will be surprised at how much you will change as you graduate and go into the workforce or college and then move on to adulthood. Friends will come and go, so will your academics, and big life decisions will be made. But one thing that can remain steady in your life is your personal relationship with the Lord. The only way to conquer inferiority is by giving it to God, and realizing that my sufficiency is from Him and Him alone. I challenge you today to remember that God created you who He wanted you to be, and for this very reason no one is better than you.

-Marie

CHALLENGE - Day 11

When someone has a dad they have something special. A dad is someone that loves you and cares for every need that you have, and strives to push you toward your greatest potential. A dad is a man that teaches you about many aspects of life. Dads give their daughters security, provide protection, show encouragement, and give guidance on things such as driving, dating, friendships, and much more. Since you are fatherless you don't have a dad to be these things to you. Whether your father has passed away or he simply lives down the street from you, there are still feelings of inferiority present. Your friends may tell you about an activity with their dad or about something their dad taught them, and this may make you feel empty and wanting for that type of relationship. This is understandable and normal in your situation. Though this feeling may never disappear completely there are steps you can take to come to grips and understand that you are fatherless. Cinderella is a fictional character that most everyone knows about. There are several variations of this story but most seem to stick to the same plot. She was a princess in her daddy's eyes and one day her father died and her wicked stepmother took over her house and her life changed forever. All Cinderella had known about life was gone. All of her confidence was taken away and now she was considered far inferior to her two stepsisters and stepmother, even to the point that she was basically a slave for them. Your story of being fatherless may feel as if it is the same as Cinderella, or you may feel it is worse or better than her situation. Regardless of how you feel, you can learn from this fictional story. No matter what your situation may be, it does not always have to stay that way. Cinderella went off and eventually married the prince. Now, you might never marry a prince, but the Bible does say that you are a child of God, who is the King of Kings (Revelation 19:16)! Many times your inferiority may be overwhelming, but if you continue on trusting God with your inferiority you will be able to live a successful life. II Corinthians 3:5 says "Not that we are sufficient of ourselves to think anything as of ourselves; but our sufficiency is of God."

 ACTION - In My Prayer Journal

Make a list of the items in your life that are lacking because of not having a dad. Then begin to pray daily that God will help you overcome your inferiority.

Suggested Prayer: Dear Lord, I give my inferiority to You. I trust You for You have made me and my sufficiency is from You. I thank You for being my confidence and my strength. Amen.

The Fatherless Journey

The Fatherless Journey
Day 12

Trusting God

"Trust in the LORD with all thine heart; and lean not unto thine own understanding.
In all thy ways acknowledge Him, and He shall direct thy paths." Proverbs 3:5-6

Do you ever struggle with trusting God with certain parts of your life? I have and when I was your age I tremendously struggled with trusting Him. I knew I was supposed to, but many times knowing and actually doing were two completely different things. Many times fatherless individuals feel that they are in a disconnect with God. Some say this is due to the lack of a manly influence on our lives, and how we view our fathers has a connection with how we view God the Father. This may be true, but it should not stop us from pursuing a close relationship with God including trusting Him with every day of our lives. I grew up fairly poor, and when it came to the point where I wanted to go to college, the financial burdens were on my shoulders. I went to the cheapest Christian college that I knew of and worked and paid my way through the first semester. Before my second semester I felt God leading me to switch to a more expensive Christian college, but I decided to lean on my own understanding and to stay at the cheaper school, and in the end I did not see God's blessing because I did not trust and obey Him. Regretfully this decision resulted in financial difficulties, because God was not in the decision that I had made. As I look back I wonder what would have happened if I would have trusted God's leading in this decision. I challenge you to trust God with your whole heart even when it seems impossible.

–Marie

CHALLENGE - Day 12

Today it seems that more and more sports players are revealing that they have a personal relationship with Jesus Christ. Many will praise God when they win a game or do something spectacular such as score a touchdown, hit a home run, make the final three pointer at the buzzer, or other remarkable events but what about when they miss the shot, lose the game, or even strike out? As fans, we hope that they will still continue to trust God with their losses just as well as their victories. As you travel along your fatherless journey there will be victories and there will be losses. Proverbs 3:5-6 gives us guidance on how we need to trust in every life circumstance. In Daniel 6, we read of how Daniel, though a faithful servant and follower of God, was cast into a lion's den. The intention for this punishment was that he would be eaten and destroyed. Even though he had been following God consistently, God allowed Daniel to go through this trial. Even in the lion's den Daniel trusted God, and this was the result: "My God hath sent His angel, and hath shut the lions' mouths, that they have not hurt me: forasmuch as before Him innocency was found in me; and also before thee, O king, have I done no hurt." Daniel 6:22. In the good times and the bad times, trust God with your life for only He can protect you!

 ACTION - In My Prayer Journal

Write out your victories and losses in life from the past month. Then write out how you could better trust God through the losses and better praise Him in the victories.

Suggested Prayer: Dear Heavenly Father, please help me today to trust You with every aspect of my life. You have created me and I trust that You will guide me through any circumstance that I may face. Amen.

The Fatherless Journey

The Fatherless Journey

Day 13

<u>Giving It All to God</u>

"It is of the LORD's mercies that we are not consumed, because His compassions fail
not. They are new every morning: great is Thy faithfulness. The LORD is my portion,
saith my soul; therefore will I hope in Him. The LORD is good unto them that wait for
Him, to the soul that seeketh Him." Lamentations 3:22-25

When I was in junior high and high school, I had friends that would give
their life to God, but this concept scared me. I was afraid that he would
call me to leave the country to be a missionary, and to me this seemed
intimidating. Then when I was 16 years old my church took a missions trip
to Mexico and through this trip I realized that being a missionary was not
as bad as I had pictured it. On this trip we worked closely with the
missionaries, helping them with different aspects of their mission work
such as painting, interacting with the children's camp, performing skits,
and a few other activities. After spending time with them it was evident
that these missionaries seemed to be filled with joy about what God had
called them to do. I realized then that when you follow God's will for your
life it is the happiest and safest place that you can be. Now that I am an
adult I would have no problem being a missionary if I knew it was His will.
As you go along your journey do not be afraid to give all of your life to
God.

-Marie

CHALLENGE - Day 13

On day 1 you were presented with Salvation and giving your heart to Jesus. Day 12 you learned about trusting God and today is about giving your life to God. Please read Romans 14:7-9 it shows us that "We are the Lord's." If you surrender to His perfect will for your life, it will be a lot easier than if you tried to go on your own life path. In Revelations 3:15-16 it says: "I know thy works, that thou art neither cold nor hot: I would thou wert cold or hot. So then because thou art lukewarm, and neither cold nor hot, I will spue thee out of my mouth." These two verses show that we as humans are either for Christ (hot) or against Christ (cold). It is better for us to be upfront about being cold or hot than to be partially for Christ and partially for the world (lukewarm). As Christians we must be on fire for Christ, there is no room nor is there any time for us to be lukewarm, and there is a punishment for this type of behavior. Being a lukewarm Christian makes Christ want to vomit. Now you have three choices that you have to pick from in your life: do you want to be cold and reject Christ, do you want to be lukewarm and make Christ vomit, or do you want to be hot and serve Christ in every area of your life? There are a multitude of examples in the Bible, throughout history, and even around you today where individuals either gave their life to God or they did not, and you and I get to learn from their examples. A famous preacher named Adrian Rogers once said, "He must be Lord of all to be Lord at all." Give your life to God today and surrender to his ultimate plan for your life.

 ## ACTION - In My Prayer Journal

Write out a letter to God telling Him the things in your life that you need and want to surrender to Him. Pray for those things that you have a hard time letting go of. Tell Him you give Him your life and really mean it.

Suggested Prayer: Dear Lord, I realize that in order for You to be Lord at all, You need to be Lord of all areas of my life. You are my Master and Creator and I give You every aspect of my life today. Thank You for constantly giving me guidance and I ask for Your strength along the rest of my journey.

The Fatherless Journey

The Fatherless Journey

Day 14

<u>Outer Beauty</u>

"For Thou hast possessed my reins: Thou hast covered me in my mother's womb. I
will praise Thee; for I am fearfully and wonderfully made: marvelous are Thy works;
and that my soul knoweth right well." Psalm 139:13-14

You are beautiful, that is right, I said you are beautiful. You are unique –
there is no one like you! I remember when I was a teenager and I felt as if
I had to keep up with the most current style. In this modern society
where women are constantly measuring themselves against Hollywood,
as if there is a perfect image that we have to achieve. We are to be thin,
perfectly fit, have flawless skin, the latest fashion, the hottest hairstyle,
and so many more demands. What people tend to overlook is that these
women are paid to have personal trainers, they have fans in front of them
when they are being photographed so that their hair is flowing flawlessly
in the breeze, their photographs are airbrushed, their bodies are fake with
Botox and plastic surgery, and much more. We all must come to realize
that everyone has flaws; I do, you do, even the most beautiful actress in
Hollywood does. That is why our verse today is so amazing. Before you
were ever thought of, God knew who you would be, what you would look
like, and He truly made you into what He wanted you to be. You are
God's blessed creation, and no one, no rude comment, nothing can
change that. God made you, He gave you hands to work, ears to hear,
eyes to see, legs to walk, a mouth to talk, and all of the other attributes of
your life, and by His ability it was all put together in a fearfully and
wonderfully made creation. I challenge you today that despite your
downfalls or shortcomings trust God and remember He made you, and
you are who He wanted you to be!

–Marie

CHALLENGE - Day 14

You were fearfully and wonderfully made (Psalm 139:13-14). That is correct; this verse is referring to you! Despite your personal criticism toward yourself and others' criticism of you; you are God's blessed creation. Despite your circumstances God made you who He wanted you to be! God has allowed this incident to occur in your life. God made you with the ability to get through this fatherless situation in your life. TLC or The Learning Channel is made up of several television programs. Many of these programs feature individuals with unique life situations that range from little people, to big people, to families with multiple children, or to people that are in need of some type of help. Imagine if they would develop a TV show that presented a different fatherless child or teen each week, it would be intriguing to see how each fatherless individual's situation is completely different. Displayed would be several similar circumstances such as hurt, pain, frustration, and inferiority. Despite what good or bad items viewers would see by watching a documentary on your life the true fact is that fearfully and wonderfully made is your design by the Ultimate Designer, God Himself. In His eyes you are a masterpiece worth more than money can buy. Always remember to praise the Lord for creating you just the way you are!

 ## ACTION - In My Prayer Journal

Write out the elements viewers would see if they watched your television show. Be honest. If there are items that you are not satisfied with, then do your best to change and then give the rest to God. Try to daily improve your "TV show" as you continue on conquering your fatherless journey!

Suggested Prayer: Dear Lord, please help me to realize and remember that I am who You made me to be. If there are items in my life that I need to change please reveal them to me and guide me to change. For the things that I cannot change due to my circumstances please help me to remember that I am fearfully and wonderfully made. Amen.

The Fatherless Journey

The Fatherless Journey

Day 15

Inner Beauty

"But the LORD said unto Samuel, Look not on his countenance, or on the height of his stature; because I have refused him: for the LORD seeth not as man seeth; for man looketh on the outward appearance, but the LORD looketh on the heart."
I Samuel 16:7

Yesterday we focused on our outer beauty; today we are going to focus on our inner beauty. I want you to really think about your inner beauty. What may make your inner person appear not so beautiful at times? Could it be jealousy, anger, bitterness, or something completely different? Even though people cannot see your inner person, God does. As a teenage girl it is easy to be jealous, angry, or even bitter toward other girls, even toward your own friends and family. When I was a teenager my father was an alcoholic and did not want to have anything to do with us, but his brother, my uncle, was the Pastor of a large Church in Las Vegas. I remember there were times when I would be somewhat jealous of my uncle's family, when comparing their home life to mine. They appeared to have what I would have called a perfect home life, and I wanted that, but if I would have let this jealousy consume me it could have ruined me. I am sure that you have viewed other home situations that you would trade with too. Jealousy is just one scenario where your inner beauty could be tainted, and remember that your inner beauty often dictates the appearance of your outer beauty, regardless of how beautiful you are on the outside. I challenge you today to not let jealousy, anger, bitterness, or anything else cause you to be ugly on the inside, because God sees it all.

-Marie

CHALLENGE - Day 15

When you see the words "inner beauty" what comes to your mind? Maybe it sparks thoughts of a friend or family member that you personally think is beautiful on the inside. Maybe it fills your mind of the attributes of a person with inner beauty, such as character, integrity, compassion, tenderhearted, etc. Maybe something completely different comes to your mind, but regardless of what comes to your mind, as a Christian the inner beauty is just as important if not more important than outer beauty. The Scripture for the day is I Samuel 16:7: "But the LORD said unto Samuel, Look not on his countenance, or on the height of his stature; because I have refused him: for the LORD seeth not as man seeth; for man looketh on the outward appearance, but the LORD looketh on the heart." The background of this passage of Scripture comes from when Samuel was commanded by God to go to Jesse to find the man that would replace Saul as King. As Samuel met with Jesse, he started with Eliab, David's older brother, but as he looked upon him the Lord told Samuel to look not on his outward appearance, because God rejected him. Obviously, God was not satisfied with the outer beauty of Eliab or David's other older brothers, but rather he saw the inner beauty of David, and that is what pleased Him. This inner beauty was the attribute that was needed to lead as the next King. This is just one example of how God favors inner beauty over outer beauty. When you begin to get ready every day, remember to focus on your inner beauty as well. Do your devotions, pray continually, be kind, be tenderhearted, and be as God would want you to be because "man looketh on the outward appearance, but the LORD looketh on the heart."

 ACTION - In My Prayer Journal

Make a list of the ways your inner beauty already shines and also the ways that it could shine brighter. Begin praying and asking God to help you to be consumed with inner beauty over outer beauty every day of your life!

Suggested Prayer: Dear Lord, help me to realize daily that You care more about my inner beauty than my outer beauty; please help me to please You by being beautiful on the inside. Amen.

The Fatherless Journey

The Fatherless Journey

Day 16

Purity of Mind and Heart

"Flee also youthful lusts: but follow righteousness, faith, charity, peace, with them that call on the Lord out of a pure heart." II Timothy 2:22

The most overlooked type of sin is that of what is in the media. We are daily surrounded with TV shows, movies, and music that tell us that adultery, swearing, being unkind to others (including murder), etc. are okay and have no consequences. We are constantly taught to be self-centered, thinking that our needs are the only thing that should matter to us. Unfortunately, these messages are only getting worse. We must realize that these things are absolutely not acceptable to God, and we must separate ourselves from them. Being fatherless meant there weren't many rules in my home. I wasted a lot of time watching TV, and I could watch whatever I wanted. As a teenager, I came to realize the effect that TV had on me and I decided to avoid it as much as possible. This change allowed me to spend more time building my relationships with friends, it kept my heart and mind clean and pure, and more importantly, it allowed for growth in my relationship with God giving me time to be still to allow Him to speak to me. It's no wonder Jesus tells us in Matthew 5:8 that the "pure in heart" will "see God." I challenge you today to examine your heart, and ask God to reveal anything that is keeping your heart and mind from purity, and remove these things from your life. This will deepen your relationship with Him!

-Marie

CHALLENGE - Day 16

A converted Indian once said the following "I have two dogs living in me - a mean dog and a good dog. They are always fighting. The mean dog wants me to do bad things, and the good dog wants me to do good things. Do you want to know which dog wins? The one I feed the most!" This statement holds true to all Christians past, present, and future. Just because you are a Christian does not mean that it is easy to be pure, and in fact, sometimes it is harder, because we are often geared to want something even more when we know that we cannot have it. We must establish a priority of living pure in our lives this will ensure that we are feeding the good dog. Philippians 4:8 says, "Finally, brethren, whatsoever things are true, whatsoever things are honest, whatsoever things are just, whatsoever things are pure, whatsoever things are lovely, whatsoever things are of good report; if there be any virtue, and if there be any praise, think on these things." If you fill your life daily with pure things such as: Scripture, prayer, good friends, wise counsel from adults, a good attitude, etc. and avoid things of the world such as: impure shows on TV, bad friends, poor counsel, lack of prayer and devotions, etc. it will bring much more happiness to your life. A good ending to add to the converted Indians story would be the following "If I continue to feed the bad dog and not the good, it will lead me down a path of destruction filled with regrets, but if I continue to feed the good dog and not the bad, it will lead me down a path of happiness filled with no regrets." Which dog will you continue to feed? If you have been feeding the bad dog, it is never too late to turn around and begin feeding the good. Feed the good dog today!

 ## ACTION - In My Prayer Journal

Make two lists, the first with ways you have been feeding the bad dog, and the second with ways that you have been feeding the good dog. Begin praying asking God to help you to only feed the good dog, eventually causing the bad dog to disappear.

Suggested Prayer: Dear Lord, please help me to have the priority of purity in my daily life. Amen.

The Fatherless Journey

THE TRIP · WEEK 2

Days 17-23

The Fatherless Journey

Day 17

Purity of Body

"But fornication, and all uncleanness, or covetousness, let it not be once named among you, as becometh saints; Neither filthiness, nor foolish talking, nor jesting, which are not convenient: but rather giving of thanks." Ephesians 5:3-4

Probably the biggest struggle as a teenager is deciding to keep yourself pure and more importantly, sticking to it. Yesterday we looked at the inward purity of mind and heart, and today we will look at what it takes to keep your body pure. As a fatherless girl, we feel a large physical void in our lives. There is no man in our lives to give us those big hugs and tell us that we are loved and protected. We are left feeling physically empty. This makes it extremely easy to want to find a way to fulfill this void by searching for it from other guys. The temptation looks lovely and the sin delicious. But the truth of the matter is you will be left feeling even worse than before: MORE unfulfilled, MORE unprotected, MORE unloved. The worst part of all this is that you are also separating yourself further from God, and you are giving up on that beautiful relationship with your Lord for completely nothing. You are sinning against your own body. Sadly, I am telling you this from experience. Because of my decision, because of my sin, I struggled for so long feeling like I did something God would never forgive me for. Maybe you are in my shoes; you've also already made mistakes in this area of your life. What's beautiful is that God DOES forgive, and you can start over with Him and purify your life! (Read Ephesians 1:7) If you have not made any impure mistakes, then guard yourselves girls, because the temptation is coming and you must be ready! One year at camp, I remember hearing a story of a girl who was being teased at public school because she was a virgin, but her peers were not. She simply turned to them and said, "Any time I want to be like you I CAN but anytime you want to be like me, you CAN'T." What a powerful statement! (Read Ephesians 5:3) I challenge you today to flee from all tempting situations, and pray hard that God will help protect you! Remind yourselves constantly of the love, fulfillment, and forgiveness that comes only from our God!

–Marie

CHALLENGE - Day 17

In today's society there are a vast variety of untrue statements being taught as truth. Young women need clarification on these lies to better understand how they can live pure with their body. Here are some of the lies that our society teaches but with true answers right beside them:

> **1. Sex Outside of Marriage is Okay – FALSE**, the Bible says that sex outside of marriage is sin. In Ephesians 5:3 and in several other passages, it clearly tells us that sex, fornication, or whatever you want to call it   is wrong, and this passage goes as far as to say that it should "not be once named among you." (See also I Corinthians 6:9-10; I Thessalonians 4:3-5; Hebrews 13:4)
>
> **2. Homosexuality is Okay – FALSE**, the Bible says in several places that homosexuality is sin. In Jude 7 it says that Sodom and Gomorrha were destroyed because of fornication and homosexuality. (See also I Corinthians 6:9-10; Deuteronomy 23:17; Leviticus 18:22; Genesis 19; Ephesians 5:31; Romans 1:24-32)
>
> **3. Abortion is Okay – FALSE**, in Exodus 20:13 the Bible says "Thou shalt not kill." Look up the word abort in a dictionary and it is the subtle word for terminate, abolish, bring to an end, cancel, conclude, cut off, etc. Regardless of what you call it, abortion is the killing of an unborn little baby, and murder is sin. (See also Ephesians 5:10-17; Galatians 5:19-21; Genesis 25:22-24; Luke 1:15; Luke 1:41-44; Ecclesiastes 11:5; Psalm 22:10)
>
> **4. Immodesty is Okay – FALSE** – The Bible says in I Timothy 2:9 that "women adorn themselves in modest apparel" this is a command. As a Christian woman, you should wear clothes that are honoring to the Lord. (See also Proverbs 11:22; Romans 14:13)
>
> **5. Please find more help on Purity at myfatherlessjourney.org.**

 # ACTION - In My Prayer Journal

Make a list of ways that you personally could live purer with your body, some examples would be pure talk, pure dress, pure thoughts, etc., and then begin striving to live them out today!

Suggested Prayer: Dear Lord, I realize that my body is not mine, but rather a temple of the Holy Ghost, please help me to live pure every day. Amen.

The Fatherless Journey

The Fatherless Journey

Day 18

Finding Godly Friendships

"Iron sharpeneth iron; so a man sharpeneth the countenance of his friend."
Proverbs 27:17

I remember in high school after giving my life to God, I started to take a look at who my close friends were. There were some who encouraged me to be a better person, to walk with God and do what was right. Then there were others who I wanted to act differently around because I was afraid of what they would think of me. Proverbs 27:10 tells us that the type of friendships we should surround ourselves with, should be ones of encouragement, ones that sharpen us to make us a better person in our walk with Christ. If you do not feel comfortable with someone enough to share with them about your relationship with God, then it is time to rethink that friendship. One problem you may encounter is that some of your friends, particularly if they were close ones, may take offense to your backing off from them. This can be a hard situation to deal with, and one that I had to encounter myself. The best way to deal with this is to pray for those friends, keep them at a distance, but not completely shun them from your life. Try to be a living example and be willing to talk to them about your new relationship with the Lord. You never know, it may allow for an opportunity to lead them to a new relationship with Christ, or it may help them to begin making better choices in their own lives. Others will disagree with you or may even mock you. No matter what happens, remember you have God on your side, and He is a friend that sticks closer than a brother! (Prov.18:24)

-Marie

CHALLENGE - Day 18

How many friends do you have? You are now probably reviewing in your mind your friends' names, and depending on your type of thought process, you may even be dividing them into different categories. There are a few different ways that you could divide up your friendships, and in this instance let us look at them in four different categories:

> **Acquaintance** – This is a friend that you may work with or go to school with, but do not really know very well and never do anything with. They should not have much influence on your life.

> **Casual** – This is a friend that you know somewhat and you talk to sometimes outside of work or school. You may even occasionally hang out with this person, probably with other friends present. They should not have much influence on your life.

> **Close** – This is a friend you spend a good bit of time with, alone or with other friends present. They know some secrets about you and you know some of theirs. These friends can be very influential in your life decisions and you theirs.

> **Best** – This is a friend you spend most of your time with. They know most of your secrets and you theirs. You love spending time with them. There will be only a few of these friends and they are one of the primary influencers in your life and you theirs.

Who are your acquaintances, casual, close, and best friends? As a Christian we must have godly friends as our best and close friends. This does not mean that you should not be casual or an acquaintance with others that do not have your same standards, but it will be harder for you to keep your standards if you surround yourself with best and close friends that do not care about them. Proverbs 27:17 shows us that we will influence and be influenced by those whom we spend our time with. Make your friendships count today!

 ## ACTION - In My Prayer Journal

Write out a list of your close and best friends. Begin praying over those friendships asking God if they are honoring to Him, and if they are not, start searching for godly friendships today!

Suggested Prayer: Dear Lord, please help me to have friendships that are honoring and pleasing to You. Please bring friends into my life that will help me walk on a straight path with You! Amen.

The Fatherless Journey

The Fatherless Journey

Day 19

Submission to Authority

"Children, obey your parents in the Lord: for this is right. Honour thy father and mother; which is the first commandment with promise; That it may be well with thee, and thou mayest live long on the earth." Ephesians 6:1-3

"Obey them that have the rule over you, and submit yourselves: for they watch for your souls, as they that must give account, that they may do it with joy, and not with grief: for that is unprofitable for you." Hebrews 13:17

My mom didn't set many rules for me as I was growing up. Of course, there was no father there to discipline me, so when my mom would ask me to do something, it was easy to not take her seriously or even tell her no. This also made it somewhat difficult with other authority (teachers, etc.). Even though I may have done what they asked me to physically, I sometimes had a really bad attitude and even got in trouble a number of times for rolling my eyes. I would even feel annoyed that anyone was telling me what to do at all. The attitudes that I had were wrong, and if I am disobedient to authority, I am also being disobedient to God. He commanded us to obey our parents and to obey all other authorities above us. I know this can be hard, but these youthful acts of obedience help train and teach us to listen to our elders all throughout life, especially to our God.

-Marie

CHALLENGE - Day 19

Authority is everywhere, regardless of your age; you will always have authority over you. Authority ranges from parents to bosses and from teachers to other adults in your life. Authority is the government, the law, and anyone placed over you in any regard. Even when you step onto an airplane for a flight you are under the authority of the flight attendant and the flight attendant is under the authority of the pilot. Typically, authority has experience that you do not possess. A man named Bill is in the United States Navy. He serves his country with dignity and honor. His service involves a multitude of duties. He is responsible to fulfill his designated job; plus, he is required to keep himself and his belongings in tip-top shape. He has to report to an officer directly above him. If one day Bill decided not to do his chores, and not to listen to his authority, there would be very large consequences to pay. He is required to live according to the standards of the United State Navy. What about you? Being a Christian, you are in the army of God. You are a Christian soldier. Part of this amazing privilege is that you must submit to the authority that is over you. On your fatherless journey strive to submit to the authority that is in your life. Romans 13:1 "Let every soul be subject unto the higher powers."

 ## ACTION - In My Prayer Journal

Write out the authority figures that are currently in your life. Then put an <u>R</u> beside the names that you feel you currently respect, and then put a <u>D</u> beside the names you are disrespectful to. Work on trying to have all <u>R</u>'s within the next 30 days, despite how hard it may be.

Suggested Prayer: Dear Lord, I ask for Your forgiveness for the disrespect that I have shown in the past, and I seek Your strength to respect and submit to the authority that You have placed and will place in my life. Amen.

The Fatherless Journey

The Fatherless Journey

Day 20

<u>Finding Security</u>

"My sheep hear My voice, and I know them, and they follow Me: And I give unto them eternal life; and they shall never perish, neither shall any man pluck them out of My hand. My Father, which gave them Me, is greater than all; and no man is able to pluck them out of My Father's hand." John 10:27-29

Since I was a little girl, I have always loved John 10:27-28. It made me feel safe and secure thinking of myself as a little sheep in the arms of the Great Shepherd. I especially love the part "neither shall any man pluck them out of my hand." Being a fatherless girl you may have experienced a lack of security at times, I know I have. One time when I was young I was staying at my grandparent's house, and it came time for me to go home. When I say home I really mean to the house that we were living at, because it was in no way a home. At the time, my mom and I were living with another guy and his son. To make a long story short, this guy was abusive both mentally and physically to my mom and me. When I had to leave my grandparent's house that night I felt like I was leaving a place of security to go back to a place where I did not feel safe at all. Eventually when I was in 11th grade we were able to move out of that unsafe house and move into my grandparent's home. Through this whole living situation, God revealed to me that He is my security. God truly is my shepherd and no matter what situation I may be in, He will protect me from the wolves, the bears, and whomever or whatever may try to harm me. I challenge you today to find your security through the Lord.

-Marie

CHALLENGE - Day 20

The following is one of the many definitions of security: "something that secures or makes safe; protection; defense."[6] Being fatherless you may often feel as if you are lacking security in your life. This is a normal feeling, but do not let a lack of security consume you, because whether you realize it or not, God is your security. God will take care of you at all times, no matter what may happen to you. Three men of great faith in the Bible were Shadrach, Meshach, and Abednego (Daniel 3) who were kidnapped from their homes and taken as slaves into a foreign country. Despite all that had happened to them they still trusted God. One day they refused to bow down to a statue of Nebuchadnezzar, because they made the decision to follow the only true God. As a result for not bowing down and worshipping the statue they were thrown into a fiery furnace. The furnace was so hot that it killed the soldiers that took Shadrach, Meshach, and Abednego to the furnace, but it was not hot enough to burn the men of God. If you read Daniel 3 it says that God was in the fire with them: "I see four men loose, walking in the midst of the fire, and they have no hurt; and the form of the fourth is like the Son of God."(vs.25) and God did not let them get harmed: "upon whose bodies the fire had no power, nor was an hair of their head singed, neither were their coats changed, nor the smell of fire had passed on them."(vs.27) Despite the fact that they were in the fiery furnace and no matter how hot it was, God provided security for them. God did not let even one hair on their head be burned nor did they smell like the fire when they came out. This is a great example of how God provides protection to us today despite the fact that you may not have a dad at home or you may not have security; trust in God to protect you and provide all of the security that you need.

 ## ACTION - In My Prayer Journal

Write a letter to God about your insecurities, and begin to trust Him to help you get through it.

Suggested Prayer: Dear Lord, I trust that You are my security. No matter how insecure I may feel, please help me to know that You are always with me and will always protect me. Amen.

The Fatherless Journey

The Fatherless Journey

Day 21

<u>Father's Day</u>

"For ye have not received the spirit of bondage again to fear; but ye have received the Spirit of adoption, whereby we cry, Abba, Father." Romans 8:15

Father's Day was always a hard day for me and my family, because we did not have a father or a daddy at home to celebrate this special day with. One day I finally learned the real meaning of Romans 8:15. One night in youth group, our pastor taught us that the Greek translation for 'Abba' literally means "Daddy." He told us that our relationship with our Heavenly Father is not just a distant formal relationship but one where we could claim Him as our very own daddy. This was an eye-opener for me! I could call someone daddy? What's more important is that we don't have to fear anything; He is always with us no matter what, and he can protect us better than any earthly father ever could be. Once we accept Jesus Christ as our personal Savior, He is ours! Daddy is a word that, if you are like me, was so unfamiliar yet one you deeply long to say, and now you can!

-Marie

CHALLENGE - Day 21

Everyone loves holidays! Most are filled with joy, happiness, and they sometimes even include a few days off of school or work. They are a time to share and reflect on the meaning of that special day. Christmas is a day to remember the Birth of Jesus Christ and Easter is when we remember His death, burial, and resurrection. Valentine's Day we take some extra time to express how we feel about the ones we like or love. On the Fourth of July we remember our independence in the United States of America and that we are free to live, and most importantly, that we have religious freedom. New Year's gives us a fresh slate to complete our goals. There are many holidays throughout the year, but one that plagues the fatherless is Father's Day. For many fatherless individuals this day brings sadness and despair. For some it might be seen somewhat too overwhelming to bear. Whatever this day brings to you, you can get through it. In Psalm 61:2, David wrote, "From the end of the earth will I cry unto Thee, when my heart is overwhelmed: lead me to the rock that is higher than I." Even David had days when he too was overwhelmed, but he trusted God to get him through those tough times. When you are feeling overwhelmed on Father's Day look to the Lord for strength and comfort. According to Roman's 8:15, we do have something to celebrate on Father's Day, our Abba Father!

 ## ACTION - In My Prayer Journal

Make a list of the reasons that Father's Day is hard for you. Pray daily that God will give you strength and comfort to get through the upcoming Father's Day and any other days that may overwhelm you.

Suggested Prayer: Dear Lord, I ask that You would please provide strength and comfort to me on Father's Day and other days that I feel overwhelmed. I realize that only through You can I get through these things, and I ask that You will lead me to the rock that is higher than I. Amen.

The Fatherless Journey

The Fatherless Journey

Day 22

Breaking the Cycle

"Then he said unto them, Go your way, eat the fat, and drink the sweet, and send portions unto them for whom nothing is prepared: for this day is holy unto our Lord: neither be ye sorry; for the joy of the LORD is your strength." Nehemiah 8:10

My mom, both of my grandma's and several aunts and uncles have told me stories of how many times my dad would get drunk, cry, and say, "my dad died when I was thirteen, and my baby died too!" While both of these cases are sad and true, it is no excuse for anyone to get drunk all of the time and to focus on themselves day after day. The crazy part is, as he is crying about these problems, he is choosing not to be a father and abandoning his 3 children that are alive. In order to have a successful future, we have to choose to let go of the bad things that have happened to us. Now I can do one of two things: I can either wallow in my sadness, choose to do wrong, and cry about my dad living on this earth and wanting nothing to do with me, or I can choose to look at his mistakes and take another path not allowing this vicious cycle to continue in the generations to come. I don't want to waste my life being sad about my misfortune, no matter how unfair it may be. Early on we talked about forgiveness. Well, a great way to gain a good perspective on this is to reflect on the following statement: "Hurt people, hurt other people." I heard this a few years back and it really opened my eyes to see what could happen if we let our problems continue to cycle through our families. I could be an unhappy person for my own children if I let bitterness take over my life and then that could cause them to hurt as well. I challenge you to pray about any "unhealed" areas of your life, and let the joy of the Lord take over your heart.

-Marie

CHALLENGE - Day 22

What is your opinion on history? Do or did you enjoy it in school? Some individuals enjoy learning history and they see the value in learning it, but others are simply not that interested. Regardless of whether you enjoy it now or not, most likely the older you will get the more interesting you will find it to be. It is filled with real life stories of war, love, peace, happiness, tragedy, and much more. Parts of history are used as examples in sermons, speeches, and presentations to clarify a specific point or topic. Many of the most popular and powerful films in Hollywood are drawn from historical events. One of the most important aspects of history is that it is a resource for all individuals to use in order to learn from examples. You can find consequences, trials, and adversity that were developed from the actions of historians. This allows us to change our methods of how we may deal with events that may happen today. Even the President of the United States looks at historical situations before he may react to a current event, because the saying is true, "hind sight sees 20/20." Which means that when you know the outcome or what the results will be from a choice or decision that you are about to make, you will have a better idea of what kind of decision to choose. I Corinthians 3:13-17 shows us that we as individuals solely answer for ourselves in God's eyes. Despite what our fathers do or have done, it is our responsibility to manage our lives according to God's will! Learn from the good and bad examples in your life to help in your decisions; break the cycle and be different.

 ## ACTION - In My Prayer Journal

Write out certain bad and good characteristics of the role models in your life, including your dad whether he is around or not. Decide that you will only model the good characteristics. Begin praying that God will help you become the woman that He wants you to be.

Suggested Prayer: Dear Lord, I pray that You will help me to model my life after Your will today. I thank You for giving me the opportunity and time to learn from examples of good and bad. Please help me to find some good examples in my life, from history, or in the Bible that I may model my life after. Amen.

The Fatherless Journey

The Fatherless Journey

Day 23

<u>Being an Example</u>

"But let every man prove his own work, and then shall he have rejoicing in himself alone, and not in another." Galatians 6:4

Although you may be fatherless, you still have the opportunity to be an example. Many individuals have a tendency to sulk about the life circumstances that they have been given, but I challenge you to stand up and be the difference in your circle of influence. I am not saying that I was always perfect, but when I was a teen God enabled me to be an example to some individuals the He brought into my life. At the beginning of my 9th grade year, there were two new girls in my class. I was able to become friends with them, and I quickly learned that they had fatherless situations just like me. Through our similar home circumstances I was able to show them that regardless of how their earthly father treated or abandoned them, they had a Heavenly Father that was waiting with His arms wide open to love them and protect them. It was exciting and encouraging that someone like me could be an example and share my faith with them. During our 9th grade year these two girls accepted Jesus Christ as their personal Savior and were able to experience God as their Heavenly Father. If you look around you, in your family, school, church, and neighborhood, there are sure to be individuals that are struggling with issues just like you. I challenge you today to let God use you as an example striving to be the leader that He created you to be.

-Marie

CHALLENGE - Day 23

In life there will be circumstances where you will need to stand and decide to be a responsible leader and example. Even though this may not have happened to you yet, there will be areas where you will be required to lead. Whether it be protecting a loved one, taking on leadership in class or at work, standing up for what is right, or something completely different, as Christians we are required to be leaders. To many individuals we may be the only Bible that they will ever read. We are to be examples of good and examples of things that are pure. We are to always be strong in displaying our faith. Hebrews 11 is often called the "faith hall of fame". It gives names such as Abel, Enoch, Noah, Abraham, Jacob, Joseph, Moses, and others. These individuals displayed leadership and were examples of strong faith in God at some point in their lives. They trusted God despite most of the bad circumstances that they may have faced. Good leadership and strong faith in God go hand in hand, just as bad leadership and living for sin do. You need to decide today whether you will be a good leader or a bad leader. Do you want to be in the faith hall of fame or the hall of shame; it is your decision. Being a bad example may be fun for a season, but nothing compares to serving God and living for Him! Galatians 6:4 tells us "But let every man prove his own work." What work have you proved or will you prove in the future. Heavenly accomplishments are the only ones that matter. Strive today to be a good example no matter what situation you are in.

 ACTION - In My Prayer Journal

Make a list of the times in your life that you currently have the opportunity to be an example. Some instances would be at school, at church, at work, etc. Then begin striving to be a godly example in these opportunities.

Suggested Prayer: Dear Lord, please help me to be the example that You would have me to be. Help me to prove my own work in the place You have currently entrusted me with and the things that will come. Amen.

The Fatherless Journey

THE TRIP - WEEK 3

Days 24-30

The Fatherless Journey

Day 24

Be Confident

"Being confident of this very thing, that He which hath begun a good work in you will perform it until the day of Jesus Christ." Philippians 1:6

People carry confidence in various ways. Some rely on natural skills they have received, others on practiced talents, and others on a mixture of the two. It is easy when you are fatherless to not feel good about yourself; however, as Christians, we should gain confidence knowing that we have Christ within us, and that our goal on earth is to fulfill the tasks that He has set aside for us to do. We don't have to try to 'succeed' in an earthly manner of speaking, because we should realize that we are here on this earth for only a short period of time, and our true purpose is to praise God and live only for Him. I always enjoyed the story of Moses and the burning bush. God appeared unto Moses and told him that He wanted him to go to Pharaoh and request that the Israelites be freed from Egypt. Moses' replies doubtfully, "Who am I to go to Pharaoh?" The Lord responds saying "Certainly I will be with thee". Yet Moses is again afraid and asks how he should describe who sent Him. The Lord says, "I AM THAT I AM...say I AM hath sent me to you." Again Moses comes to God with an excuse of "they will not believe me" and "I am not eloquent...I am slow of speech." (I can relate to this one!) (Exodus 3:1- 4:17) Excuses, excuses, it is easy to think of reasons why we can't do things for God, and much of it is driven by self-consciousness. I find myself doing this even now. We must realize that God started His will with you and He will equip you with the abilities necessary to fulfill His tasks. I challenge you today to be confident in all you do!

-Marie

CHALLENGE - Day 24

Abraham Lincoln was a great man. Not only was he a great president, but he also is given credit for the abolition of slavery in the United States. Despite his great accomplishments and prestigious positions, honest Abe was not always a success. In fact, he had run for the United States Senate on two occasions and did not win. At this time in his life, he was probably feeling defeated and he probably had a lack of confidence. Despite all of the great things he accomplished later in life, these losses were probably very discouraging. Despite his failures he remained confident, though it was probably not easy and eventually became the President of the United States. [7] Sometimes you may feel overwhelmed and not have any confidence at all, but there is hope. Luke 1:37 shows us that "For with God nothing shall be impossible." God created this earth. He created it and is the master of everything. He is our Guide, our Deliverer, and our Strength. He sent His Son to die for our sins on the cross to save us from an eternity in Hell. He is Almighty, All Powerful. Be confident in the Lord for His grace is sufficient. Trust God today and let Him alone be your confidence.

 ## ACTION - In My Prayer Journal

Make a list of the top 10 things in your life that seem to be impossible. Begin praying for these things daily until they are no longer impossible.

Suggested Prayer: Dear Lord, I put my trust in You. Please help me to be confident in You in the good and the bad times. I trust You with my life, and only through You am I able to move forward each day. Amen.

The Fatherless Journey

The Fatherless Journey

Day 25

<u>Mentors</u>

"For the LORD God is a sun and shield: the LORD will give grace and glory: no good thing will He withhold from them that walk uprightly." Psalm 84:11

I have often thought of what it would have been like if my birth dad would never have left. I wonder where I would be if he would have been the masculine influence on my upbringing. Since my father struggles with several different addictions and was very abusive verbally and physically, it would have hindered my ability to grow up as well as I did. I am not saying that I am perfect, but if I would have had his influence on my life I may be addicted, abused, and even abusive myself. I am truly grateful that God did not allow this to happen, but instead He brought men and women into my life to be my mentors. Although nothing compares to actually having a father of your own there is a lot that can be learned by seeking out godly mentors. Fortunately for me, my youth leaders knew my home situation and took me under their wing as best as they could. Spending as much time with them as possible helped me realize my future was not set by the choices my parents made, but rather it was all up to me. By keeping a close relationship with God, you too can have a successful future. I challenge you today to pray and search for a godly mentor.

-Marie

CHALLENGE - Day 25

Even though you are fatherless, in every situation there is always a positive element that needs to be addressed: mentors. One of the most interesting parts of being fatherless is that you get to have mentors. What truly is a mentor? A definition of a good mentor would be the following: A godly influence that one is able to watch, imitate, and gain knowledge from in a positive manner; filling the void of being a fatherless individual. Whether direct or indirect a mentor helps grow the individual in the right path of life. Let me tell you about a boy named George. When George was eleven years old his father died. George is a man that every American has heard of. He accomplished great things in his life time. This boy later became known as the Father of the United States of America: George Washington. Everyone has seen this great man's face on either the quarter or a one dollar bill. Despite the fatherless journey in George Washington's life he still had great success. One of the keys to George Washington's success was that he had a mentor in his life. After his father died his older half-brother became a hero and mentor to him.[8] Just like George Washington, you too need to seek for a mentor in your life. A godly mentor will help you make the right decisions, provide encouragement, and simply will be there for you. Begin praying today, asking God that He may provide a mentor for you, and if you already have a mentor, thank God for them!

 # ACTION - In My Prayer Journal

Make a list of the characteristics that you would look for in a mentor. For example, you may want a person that will teach you about life, about driving, etc. Begin praying, asking God to provide a mentor that you can model your life after.

Suggested Prayer: Dear Lord, I ask that You will bring into my life a Christian that will teach me life lessons that I have not yet learned, and that will challenge me to live a life that is honoring and pleasing to You. Amen.

The Fatherless Journey

The Fatherless Journey

Day 26

A Biblical Marriage

"Two are better than one; because they have a good reward for their labour. For if they fall, the one will lift up his fellow: but woe to him that is alone when he falleth; for he hath not another to help him up." Ecclesiastes 4:9-10

I remember a message that our youth pastor preached to us a few times when I was a teenager entitled, "7 Steps to Perfect Dating." While all of the steps were helpful tools in dating and seeking out a mate, there was a particular step that stuck out to me the most. That step was "Don't look for the right one, be the right one and you'll find the right one." This is so important especially when considering marriage. So many marriages today don't have much thought put into them. People get married possibly out of loneliness and some on a whim mistaking infatuation for true love. They don't realize the lifetime commitment ahead of them, and after being married for some time, those feelings may die off and sometimes end in a life of unhappiness or even divorce. Unfortunately, without a dad, it is easy to go after the wrong person. You need to understand just how important it is to be with the right one. God created marriage to be a special union and He has the perfect person picked out for you; trust Him with this. It may seem odd, but I challenge you to start praying now for your future husband, ultimately for his personal walk with God, and then only take steps toward finding him by being the right person yourself.

-Marie

CHALLENGE - Day 26

What are your thoughts on marriage? Just after reading that question something came to your mind, but did your thoughts reflect a Biblical view of marriage? In today's society many individuals have a twisted view of marriage. There are several examples of what our society teaches us about marriage, but as a Christian you must have a Biblical view of it. In Genesis 2:18,21-24 we see the first marriage that ever took place on the face of the earth. God created marriage and we as humans have no authority to change what the Lord established. The ideal situation would be for you to experience and watch how a healthy couple such as a mother and father get along and interact with one another, but you have to accept what you have been given. God will bring couples into your life that will be godly examples for you, and you can pick the pieces out of each of their relationships of how you think a marriage should be. When you are dating a guy, remember that you belong to God and not your boyfriend or fiancé. No man should act as if he has ownership of you, and if this happens, end the relationship right away. Sex is something God created for married couples and married couples only. Whatever man God brings into your life, the following are a few guidelines you can follow:

> 1. Put God first – God should always be the first priority in your life.
> 2. Respect him – He is not your possession; he belongs to God, and the same goes with how he views you.
> 3. Pray – Pray daily for the man that God will have you marry.
> 4. Read the Bible – Seek God's will through His Scriptures.
> 5. Don't rush anything – "Your body is the temple of the Holy Ghost." (I Corinthians 6:19)

 # ACTION - In My Prayer Journal

Write out a description of your ideal husband. Remember to include his desire to serve God, his appearance, his abilities, his strengths, his personality traits, and whatever else that may come to your mind that reflects a man of God. Begin praying daily for this man, asking God to prepare both you and him for your future life together.

Suggested Prayer: Dear Lord, please help me to be a woman that is honoring and pleasing to You. Please guide me to the man that You will have me to marry, and prepare us for each other. Only through You am I able to find the man that You want me to have. Amen.

The Fatherless Journey

The Fatherless Journey

Day 27

Finding Wisdom

"If any of you lack wisdom, let him ask of God, that giveth to all men liberally, and upbraideth not; and it shall be given him." James 1:5

Many people often think of knowledge and wisdom as the same thing. However, wisdom is actually a deeper form of knowledge that can only truly come by seeking it from God. Although we can seek wisdom from God on a daily basis through prayer and Bible study, fasting is a great way too. The summer before I went to college, I was very confused about what I should do. I had two choices: stay home and work a job in town and then go to college or live at the college for the summer and work for the school. The job at college would be free room and board and pay for my tuition for my first semester. I took a day of fasting and prayer seeking wisdom for which choice to make. After this time I had complete peace about going to college early and working there, and that same day I applied for the summer program. On a side note, I was accepted to the program and my three other friends that applied were not. Not to say that I was any better than my friends that applied, but that it was God's will for me to be hired. God provided wisdom when I needed it. I challenge you today to seek wisdom from God for only through Him will you find it!

-Marie

CHALLENGE - Day 27

The World English Dictionary defines wisdom as the following: "accumulated knowledge, erudition, or enlightenment."[9] This basically means that wisdom is something that is gained. A few definitions of wisdom from the Bible are the following: "the price of wisdom is above rubies" (Job 28:18), "Wisdom is the principal thing; therefore get wisdom: and with all thy getting get understanding." (Proverbs 4:7), and "wisdom giveth life to them that have it." (Ecclesiastes 7:12). During Bible times, all throughout history and even until today, wisdom has been set as one of the most valuable things that one might possess. Today, wisdom is something that you will earn through the years of your life, but for Solomon this was not the case. In I Kings 3 it shows us that one night God appeared to Solomon through a dream and God asked Solomon, "Ask what I shall give thee."(vs.5) this was an open question from God allowing Solomon to ask for ANYTHING! What would you have asked for? Be honest, you thought of one, two, or maybe three things. Solomon knew that he needed guidance above anything else, so he asked God for wisdom, and in verse 10 it says that God was pleased with Solomon's decision. Not only did God give wisdom to Solomon, but He gave him riches, honor, and if he kept God's commandments he would have a long life too. Today, Christian's do not always have to earn wisdom, as our dictionary definition above suggests, but rather in many circumstances it can be obtained by praying for it. Do not waste your opportunity to possess wisdom today for it "is above rubies."

 # ACTION - In My Prayer Journal

Write out some questions, problems, or issues that are in your life right now where you are lacking wisdom. Pray for these things that God will provide the wisdom that you need.

Suggested Prayer: Dear Lord, please give me wisdom and guidance daily to make decisions that are honoring to You! Amen.

The Fatherless Journey

The Fatherless Journey

Day 28

Woman of God

"Nevertheless the foundation of God standeth sure, having this seal, The Lord knoweth them that are His. And, Let everyone that nameth the name of Christ depart from iniquity." II Timothy 2:19

Being fatherless, I grew up with the option to decide who I wanted to be. I could be like movie stars, teachers, artists, musicians, or a multitude of different other people. While I was on the fatherless journey, I soon realized that everyone that did not have a relationship with Christ, for the most part, were living empty lives. They were famous or successful for some earthly reason, but the true happiness and meaning were absent. The true heroes in my life became the godly men and women around me. They were heroes, to a point, because they were giving me the example of how to be a Woman of God myself. A few traits that I have found to be common amongst women of God are: patience, kindness, love, tenderhearted, boldness in Christ, constant in prayer, slow to anger, God fearing, pure, consistent, forgiving, and many others. Now I am not saying you will have the characteristics overnight, but they are something to strive for. A good place to start to learn how to be a woman of God is to study about the Proverbs 31 woman. Proverbs 31:10 tells us that a virtuous woman's price is far above rubies. It goes further to say that she is selfless, hardworking, full of wisdom, kind, trustworthy, and fears God. In return she is praised by her children, husband, and God. We will not ever be perfect on this earth, but life is filled with hope and joy when we strive to truly be women of God. I challenge you today to strive to be a woman of God.

-Marie

CHALLENGE - Day 28

Have you ever read about Job in the Bible or heard his story in church or in a Sunday School class? Often it is easy for our imaginations to group Biblical individuals as "Bible Characters" just as Mickey Mouse or Bugs Bunny are "Disney Characters." It may be because we refer to them as "characters" or it may be that we consider them to be cartoons instead of once living. Job was a real person just like you; he was not a fictional character in any way, but a true, real man of God. His story is amazing and many of us could not even begin to imagine going through what he did in such a short time. He lost his children, health, wealth, and dignity all in a matter of hours. Despite it all, he was still a man of God. Despite his own wife telling him to curse God and die, he was still a man of God. He knew that God had allowed these things to happen for a reason. Just like Job strived to be a man of God, we need to strive to be women of God despite anything that you may be facing in your life.

 ACTION - In My Prayer Journal

Write out anything that comes between you and God. Examples would be possessions, friends, sin, entertainment, or a variety of other things. Pray that God would help you to overcome these things and that He will help you to grow daily as a woman of God.

Suggested Prayer: Dear Lord, help me today to live for You. Please give me strength to resist temptation and to follow You despite what challenges may come into my life. I want to be a woman of God today and for the rest of my life. Amen.

The Fatherless Journey

The Fatherless Journey

Day 29

Setting Goals

"Delight thyself also in the LORD; and He shall give thee the desires of thine heart.
Commit thy way unto the LORD; trust also in Him; and He shall bring it to pass."
Psalm 37:4-5

A hymn I remember as a fatherless child went like this:

"Have Thine own way, Lord! Have Thine own way! Thou art the Potter, I am the clay. Mold me and make me after Thy will, While I am waiting, yielded and still. Have Thine own way, Lord! Have Thine own way! Search me and try me, Master, today! Whiter than snow, Lord, wash me just now, As in Thy presence humbly I bow. Have Thine own way, Lord! Have Thine own way! Wounded and weary, help me, I pray! Power, all power, surely is Thine! Touch me and heal me, Savior divine. Have Thine own way, Lord! Have Thine own way! Hold o'er my being absolute sway! Fill with Thy Spirit 'till all shall see Christ only, always, living in me."[10]

Many times people think that Psalm 37:4-5 is saying when you do right, God will give you anything that you desire. However, when I was in youth group one night, we learned that to "Delight thyself also in the Lord" is to be moldable or pliable, and that when you allow yourself to be created in God's image and commit your life to Him, He will then "give thee the desires of thine heart." This means that He will reveal the plan that He has for you and you will be excited to fulfill it. Your desire will also be the same as His plan for your life. When you are dreaming about your future remember to stay close to God and be willing to let Him mold your life into what He wants it to be.

-Marie

CHALLENGE - Day 29

Everyone has goals in life: some have good goals, some have bad goals, some have a lot of goals, some have few goals, some have set high goals, and some have set mediocre goals. What kind of goals have you set for yourself so far in your life? Setting goals is very important to a successful life journey. You do not have to know what you want to be in the future, what next year will bring, or even what will take place next month, but you should still set goals for the immediate and long-term future. For example, planning or purposing in your heart that you will do your best in school before it starts each day is a way of setting an immediate goal. Deciding that you will be pure each day and purposing that this will not change until your wedding day is an example of both an immediate and a long-term goal. Praying and asking God to open your heart and teach you something before church is an example of setting an immediate goal. Setting goals is deciding in the present how you want your life to be in the future. Sometimes your goals may not turn out exactly how you imagined, but as long as you are delighting in the Lord and committing your life to Him, He will guide you to the life He wants you to have. Pray and ask God today to help you establish goals that are honoring to Him.

 ## ACTION - In My Prayer Journal

Begin making a list of goals for the next month, year, or even five years. Make goals on living pure, succeeding in school, respecting your parents, growing as a Christian, and whatever else the Lord leads you to.

Suggested Prayer: Dear Lord, please help me today to establish goals in my life that are honoring and pleasing to You. Help me to please You with the life which You have given to me. Amen.

The Fatherless Journey

The Fatherless Journey

Day 30

Success

"Whether therefore ye eat, or drink, or whatsoever ye do, do all to the glory of God." I Corinthians 10:31

Congratulations! You made it! Today is the last day on the path to conquering your fatherless journey, and I want to be the first to congratulate you! You have done a great job, and I am very proud of you! You are on your way to having the ability to live a successful life! I am so excited that you made it. I am sure you will agree that working through these issues was not the easiest thing that you have done, but they needed to be accomplished. In the future you may even have to remind yourself of God's love and strength to get you through a difficulty in life. I am proud of you for completing this devotional and sticking to it. A great life application verse is I Thessalonians 5:24 "Faithful is He that calleth you, Who also will do it." Success is completing what you have committed to: whether it be a job, relationship, chore, or whatever it may be if you commit to something strive to complete it. Today, I am a mom; I am still working on my Psychology Degree, and I am trying to develop my musical abilities. God is still calling me to do things that I did not realize that I was going to do, and He has given me the courage and abilities to fulfill them as I walk. I challenge you today to continue on a successful path along your fatherless journey.

-Marie

CHALLENGE - Day 30

Noah's Ark and the story of the Flood have become known throughout the world. For many it is an intriguing story that people look at as fiction. Noah was a real man, and the flood that covered the earth actually did happen. Maybe they cannot comprehend giving of their lives to God to build an Ark that took several years. Maybe they cannot comprehend the fact that every man besides Noah's family was wiped off the face of the earth. It could be that they do not understand how one could save at least two of every kind of animal or that a boat could be built back then that would make it through such a storm. There are many things concerning Noah's journey, the construction of the ark and the actual flood, that we may have a hard time understanding. Noah probably struggled with understanding it as well, but in the end, it was a success. Noah was not perfect, but he did what God had told him to do. He took the burden of a large problem upon his shoulders, and this is what Hebrews 11:7 says about him: "By faith Noah, being warned of God of things not seen as yet, moved with fear, prepared an ark to the saving of his house; by the which he condemned the world, and became heir of the righteousness which is by faith." What about you? Right now your flood is your fatherless situation, and you must not give up as you build the big boat to survive. You have to continue on with the project until it is completed. At Life Factors Ministries we are praying that you will grow strong in the Lord as you continue on in your fatherless journey.

 ## ACTION - In My Prayer Journal

Write out the things that you will need to continue to work through on your fatherless journey so that you will have true success. Pray, asking God to give you wisdom and guidance along your journey.

Suggested Prayer: Dear Lord, I thank You for giving me the ability to finish this devotional and life guide. I thank You for the lessons that You have taught me and I ask that You would please help me to live a successful life according to Your will. Amen.

The Fatherless Journey

MYFATHERLESSJOURNEY.ORG

MYFATHERLESSJOURNEY.ORG

Life Factors Ministries created myfatherlessjourney.org as a website specifically designed to meet the needs of all fatherless girls/guys, single moms/guardians, and mentors. We are here for you and want to help you along your fatherless journey! Check out the site today!

MY PRAYER JOURNAL

MY PRAYER JOURNAL

_____

NAME

The Fatherless Journey

PRAYER JOURNAL INTRODUCTION

Every day of the fatherless journey you
will be asked to take action and make
an entry into this prayer journal. This
journal will help you on your journey
in many ways. After you have
completed your 30 day fatherless
journey you should refer back to your
journal to watch the progress that you
have been making in your life. As you
will notice, as you go through this
fatherless journey that prayer and
trusting God are the most important
tools that you will ever use.

The Fatherless Journey

TRIP SCHEDULE

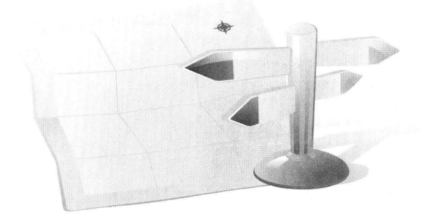

Preparation

Day 1 – Your Heavenly Father

Day 2 – So, You Are Fatherless

Day 3 – Facing the Facts

Day 4 – Talking to God

Day 5 – You Are Not Alone

Day 6 – You Are Loved

Day 7 – Consequences for Not Going

Day 8 – Overcoming Fear

Day 9 – Dealing with Discouragement

The Trip – Week 1 – The Beginning (Internal Change)

Day 10 – Forgiveness

Day 11 – Inferiority

Day 12 – Trusting God

Day 13 – Giving It All to God

Day 14 – Outer Beauty

Day 15 – Inner Beauty

Day 16 – Purity of Mind and Heart

The Trip – Week 2 – The Middle (External Change)

Day 17 – Purity of Body
Day 18 – Finding Godly Friendships
Day 19 – Submission to Authority
Day 20 – Finding Security
Day 21 – Father's Day
Day 22 – Breaking the Cycle
Day 23 – Being an Example

The Trip – Week 3 – The End (Your Future)

Day 24 – Be Confident
Day 25 – Mentors
Day 26 – A Biblical Marriage
Day 27 – Finding Wisdom
Day 28 – Woman of God
Day 29 – Setting Goals
Day 30 – Success

My Prayer Journal

Day 1 – Your Heavenly Father

John 3:16

 ACTION

In your first prayer journal entry, write out a thank you letter to God for sending His Son to die for your sins.

My Prayer Journal

Day 2 – So, You Are Fatherless

Philippians 4:11

 ### ACTION

Write out the things that you have to be thankful for and content about in your life. Remember that your life can always be in a worse position than it currently is.

My Prayer Journal

Day 3 – Facing the Facts

Jeremiah 29:11

 ACTION

Write out a challenge for yourself of how you will not become one of the statistics. Challenge yourself with goals that can be easily accomplished. Continuously look back at your goals and confirm that you are still accomplishing them.

My Prayer Journal

Day 4 – Talking to God

James 5:16b

 ACTION

Write a note to God thanking Him for the things He has done and is doing in your life. Talk to Him about your burdens and problems. Look back at this note often and see what God has done in your life.

My Prayer Journal

Day 5 – You Are Not Alone

Hebrews 13:5

 ACTION

Make a list of the times you feel most alone. Begin to ask God to give you strength and comfort in those times.

My Prayer Journal

Day 6 – You Are Loved

Galatians 2:20

 ACTION

Write a letter to Jesus thanking Him for His love and for what He has done in your life.

My Prayer Journal

Day 7 – Consequences for Not Climbing
Ephesians 5:14-17

 ACTION

Make a list of the top 5 things that you know God wants you to do with your life right now. Some examples would be: respecting your parents, conquering this journey, living a pure life, giving 100% in school, witnessing to a friend, quitting a bad habit, etc.

My Prayer Journal

Day 8 – Overcoming Fear

II Timothy 1:7

 ACTION

Write out a list of all of your fears. Begin meditating on II Timothy 1:7 daily thinking of your fears, and ask God to help you conquer them.

My Prayer Journal

Day 9 – Dealing with Discouragement

Psalm 55:22

 ACTION

Make a list of the items you are currently discouraged about in your life.
Pray over them and then begin praying for 30 days straight that God would
deliver you from discouragement.

My Prayer Journal

Day 10 - Forgiveness

Ephesians 4:31-32

 ACTION

Make a list of the individuals in your life that you need to forgive. Begin to pray for them and ask God to forgive you for any bitterness, hatred, or anger that you may feel. Then daily seek his strength and guidance to love those that have hurt you.

My Prayer Journal

Day 11 - Inferiority

II Corinthians 3:5

 ACTION

Make a list of the items in your life that are lacking because of not having a dad. Then begin to pray daily that God will help you overcome your inferiority.

My Prayer Journal

Day 12 – Trusting God

Proverbs 3:5-6

 ACTION

Write out your victories and losses in life from the past few months. Then write out how you could better trust God through the losses and better praise Him in the victories.

My Prayer Journal

Day 13 - Giving It All to God

Lamentations 3:22-25

 ACTION

Write out a letter to God telling Him the things in your life that you need and want to surrender to Him. Pray for those things that you have a hard time letting go of. Tell Him you give Him your life and really mean it.

My Prayer Journal

Day 14 – Outer Beauty

Psalm 139:13-14

 ACTION

Write out the elements viewers would see if they watched your television show. Be honest. If there are items that you are not satisfied with, then do your best to change and then give the rest to God. Try to daily improve your "TV show" as you continue on conquering your fatherless journey!

My Prayer Journal

Day 15 – Inner Beauty

I Samuel 16:7

 ACTION

Make a list of the ways your inner beauty already shines and also the ways that it could shine brighter. Begin praying and asking God to help you to be consumed with inner beauty over outer beauty every day of your life!

My Prayer Journal

Day 16 – Purity of Heart and Mind

II Timothy 2:22

 ACTION

Make two lists, the first with ways you have been feeding the bad dog, and the second with ways that you have been feeding the good dog. Begin praying asking God to help you to only feed the good dog, eventually causing the bad dog to disappear.

My Prayer Journal

Day 17 – Purity of Body

Ephesians 5:3-4

 ACTION

Make a list of ways that you personally could live purer with your body, some examples would be pure talk, pure dress, pure thoughts, etc., and then begin striving to live them out today!

My Prayer Journal

Day 18 – Finding Godly Friendships

Proverbs 27:17

 ACTION

Write out a list of your close and best friends. Then begin praying over those friendships asking God if they are honoring to Him, and if they are not, start searching for godly friendships today!

My Prayer Journal

Day 19 – Submission to Authority
Ephesians 6:1-3 & Hebrews 13:17

 ACTION

Write out the authority figures that are currently in your life. Then put an <u>R</u>
beside the names that you feel you currently respect, and then put a <u>D</u>
beside the names you are disrespectful to. Work on trying to have all <u>R</u>'s
within the next 30 days, despite how hard it may be.

My Prayer Journal

Day 20 – Finding Security

John 10:27-29

 ACTION

Write a letter to God about your insecurities, and begin to trust Him to help you get through it.

My Prayer Journal

Day 21 – Father's Day

Romans 8:15

 ACTION

Make a list of the reasons that Father's Day is hard for you. Pray daily that God will give you strength and comfort to get through the upcoming Father's Day and any other days that may overwhelm you.

My Prayer Journal

Day 22 – Breaking the Cycle

Nehemiah 8:10

 ACTION

Write out certain bad and good characteristics of the role models in your life, including your dad whether he is around or not. Decide that you will only model the good characteristics. Begin praying that God will help you become the woman that He wants you to be.

My Prayer Journal

Day 23 – Being an Example

Galatians 6:4

 ## ACTION

Make a list of the times in your life that you currently have the opportunity to be an example. Some instances would be at school, at church, at work, etc. Then begin striving to be a godly example in these opportunities.

My Prayer Journal

Day 24 – Be Confident

Philippians 1:6

 ACTION

Make a list of the top 10 things in your life that seem to be impossible. Begin praying for these things daily until they are no longer impossible.

My Prayer Journal

Day 25 – Mentors

Psalm 84:11

 ACTION

Make a list of the characteristics that you would look for in a mentor. For example, you may want a person that will teach you about life, how to drive, etc. Begin praying, asking God to provide a mentor that you can model your life after.

My Prayer Journal

Day 26 – A Biblical Marriage

Ecclesiastes 4:9-10

 ACTION

Write out a description of your ideal husband. Remember to include his desire to serve God, his appearance, his abilities, his strengths, his personality traits, and whatever else that may come to your mind that reflects a man of God. Begin praying daily for this man, asking God to prepare both you and him for your future life together.

My Prayer Journal

Day 27 – Find Wisdom

James 1:5

 ACTION

Write out some questions, problems, or issues that are in your life right now where you are lacking wisdom. Pray for these things that God will provide the wisdom that you need.

My Prayer Journal

Day 28 - Woman of God

II Timothy 2:19

 ACTION

Write out anything that comes between you and God. Examples would be possessions, friends, sin, entertainment, or a variety of other things. Pray that God would help you to overcome these things and that He will help you to grow daily as a woman of God.

My Prayer Journal

Day 29 – Setting Goals

Psalm 37:4-5

 ACTION

Begin making a list of goals for the next month, year, or even five years. Make goals on living pure, succeeding in school, respecting your parents, growing as a Christian, and whatever else the Lord leads you to.

My Prayer Journal

Day 30 - Success

I Corinthians 10:31

 ACTION

Write out the things that you will need to continue to work through on your fatherless journey so that you will have true success. Pray, asking God to give you wisdom and guidance along your journey.

MYFATHERLESSJOURNEY.ORG
MYFATHERLESSJOURNEY.ORG

Life Factors Ministries created myfatherlessjourney.org as a website specifically designed to meet the needs of all fatherless girls/guys, single moms/guardians, and mentors. We are here for you and want to help you along your fatherless journey! Check out the site today!

NOTES

1. U.S. Dept. of Justice, Special Report, Sept 1988.

2. McLanahan, Sara and Gary Sandefur. *Growing up with a Single Parent: What Hurts, What Helps*. (Cambridge: Harvard University Press, 1994).

3. U.S. Department of Health and Human Services, National Center for Health Statistics, Survey on Child Health, Washington, DC, 1993.

4. "Gilligan's Island Theme Song," http://www.lyricsmode.com/lyrics/g/gilligans_island/gilligans_island_theme_song.html.

5. "Todd Beamer," http://en.wikipedia.org/wiki/Todd_Beamer.

6. "Security," http://dictionary.reference.com/browse/security. 17 February 2011.

7. "Abraham Lincoln," http://en.wikipedia.org/wiki/Abraham_Lincoln.

8. Joseph J. Ellis, *His Excellency: George Washington* (New York: Vintage Books, 2004). 7-10.

9. "Wisdom." World English Dictionary on Dictionary.com. HarperCollins Publishers. 2009. 17 February 2011.

10. "Have Thine Own Way Lord," http://www.hymnlyrics.org/mostpopularhymns/have_thine_own_way_lord.php.

CPSIA information can be obtained at www.ICGtesting.com
Printed in the USA
LVOW042129191011

251299LV00003B/3/P